# A History of Germs

# THE GERM DETECTIVES

 By Jim Ollhoff

Published by ABDO Publishing Company, 8000 West 78th Street, Suite 310, Edina, MN 55439. Copyright ©2010 by Abdo Consulting Group, Inc. International copyrights reserved in all countries. No part of this book may be reproduced in any form without written permission from the publisher. ABDO & Daughters™ is a trademark and logo of ABDO Publishing Company.

Printed in the United States.

♻ PRINTED ON RECYCLED PAPER

**Editor:** John Hamilton
**Graphic Design:** Sue Hamilton
**Cover Design:** John Hamilton
**Cover Photo:** Photo Researchers
**Interior Photos and Illustrations:** AP-pg 29; Corbis-pgs 13, 16, & 28; Getty Images-pgs 6 & 29; The Granger Collection-pgs 5, 9, 21, 24, & 26; iStockphoto-pg 3; Jupiterimages-pgs 4, 12, 17, 19, 21, & 27; Library of Congress-pg 14; Photo Researchers-pgs 1, 2, 10, 20, 22, 25, & 27; University of Delaware-pg 11, Wikimedia-7 & 11 .

Library of Congress Cataloging-in-Publication Data

Ollhoff, Jim, 1959-
  The germ detectives / Jim Ollhoff.
     p. cm. – (A history of germs)
  Includes index.
  ISBN 978-1-60453-499-3
  1. Bacteria–Juvenile literature. 2. Microbiologists–Juvenile literature. 3. Microbiology–Juvenile literature.  I. Title.

  QR74.8.O45 2010
  616.9'041092–dc22

                    2008055062

# CONTENTS

# THE GERM DETECTIVES

**T**oday, everyone knows that germs cause many diseases. That's why people wash their hands. It's why people clean their kitchen counters, and it's why houses have sewer systems. And when people get sick today, they can usually go to the doctor and get medicine that kills the germs.

For most of human history, people didn't know what caused disease. The knowledge of germs has only been around for about 150 years. Before that time, people couldn't see germs, because there were no microscopes. So, they blamed disease on many things—on bad air, or witchcraft, or punishment from God, or any number of reasons.

By the 1800s, doctors began to move away from superstitious ideas of disease. They began to suspect that something else was at work. They started to experiment with other ideas. A string of scientists began to lead the way out of ideas of black magic and bad air. These scientists pursued new and creative ideas. They fought for their ideas, and risked their reputations on the radical idea that germs caused disease. Today, we have a better understanding of disease because of the pioneering work of these germ detectives.

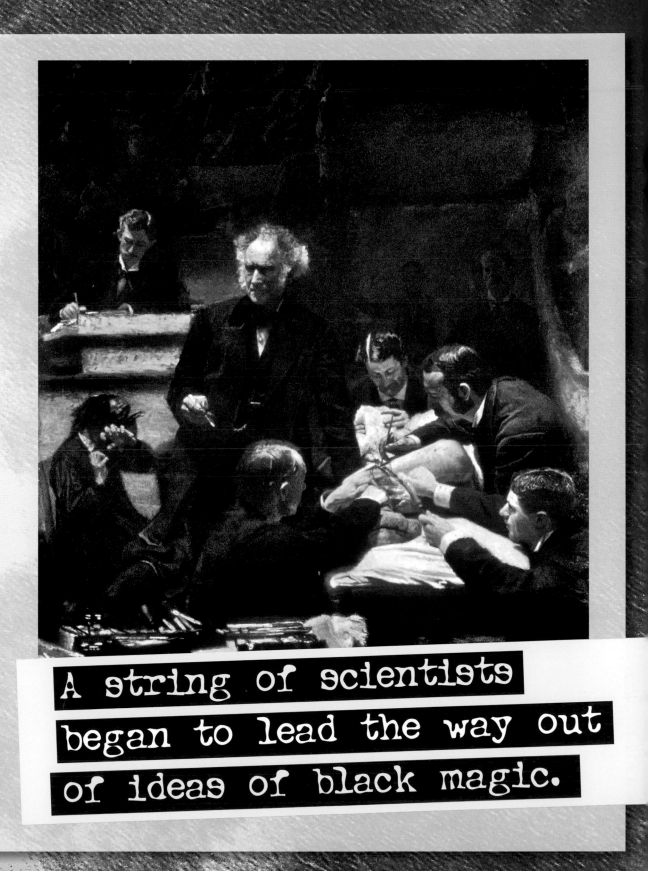

A string of scientists began to lead the way out of ideas of black magic.

# TOO MUCH BLOOD?

**M**ost early views of disease centered on religious causes. Disease, the ancients believed, resulted from evil spirits. The earliest known surgery, called *trepanation,* dates back several thousand years, and is found in many different cultures. It involved drilling holes in people's skulls, possibly to let "evil spirits" escape. Astonishingly, some people survived the operation.

Hippocrates, a Greek philosopher, is considered to be the father of medicine. He was one of the first people to disagree with the then-common belief that people became ill because of evil spirits.

A common ancient view of disease began during the days of the Greek philosophers Hippocrates (460–370 BC) and Galen (129–200 AD). According to their view, the human body had four fluids: blood, phlegm, yellow bile, and black bile. When those fluids, called humors, were in balance, a person remained healthy. If the humors got out of balance, then a person got sick. It was the job of the physician to get the humors back into balance. Because people had more blood than the other fluids, physicians usually believed that "too much blood" caused illness.

The earliest known surgery was called trepanation. It involved drilling holes in people's skulls, possibly to let evil spirits escape.

A fleam allowed the doctor to choose what size lancet to use for bloodletting.

Bleeding, or bloodletting, was done in a variety of ways. Sometimes, leeches were used. But more often, physicians used precise surgical instruments. One such instrument was called a lancet, which quickly made small incisions on a person's skin. The blood would then be collected in a shallow bowl. Another method of bloodletting was to place a glass cup against the skin, and then heat it with a flame. This created a blood-filled blister, which the physician would then cut. In the 1700s and 1800s in Europe, even healthy people allowed doctors to drain their blood. They believed bloodletting actually prevented sickness!

Of course, the draining of blood only made people sicker, and it ran the risk of causing infection. Even though bloodletting didn't work, physicians still performed the procedure. Bloodletting made sense to doctors because of the way they understood disease, so they continued the practice because they believed it *should* work.

The theory of bloodletting had different variations through the years. An American physician named Benjamin Rush, a signer of the Declaration of Independence, believed in a theory related to bloodletting. Too much blood, he thought, didn't cause disease. It was caused by nervous energy. He believed nervous energy was caused by too much buildup in the intestines. So he gave people medicines that caused violent diarrhea. Again, this made people sicker, and could even be fatal because of dehydration. But like other doctors, he stubbornly held on to his beliefs.

By the end of the 1800s, the practice of bloodletting was falling out of style. A number of discoveries added to the medical understanding of disease. Germ theory, the idea that germs cause disease, was slowly becoming more popular.

In the 1700s and 1800s in Europe, even healthy people allowed doctors to drain their blood. They believed this would prevent them from getting sick.

# A DISEASE OF TINY CREATURES

The idea that tiny creatures might cause disease had been around for a long time, even though most educated people dismissed the notion. The Roman writer Marcus Terentius Varro (116 BC – 27 BC) wrote a book about agriculture. He warned people not to build houses near swamps, because those areas "breed certain minute creatures which cannot be seen by the eyes, but which float in the air and enter the body through the mouth and nose and cause serious diseases." Even though people knew that diseases such as malaria were more common in swampland, Varro's ideas were way ahead of his time.

Even before the Roman era, people knew that a person who had a disease could transmit it to another. People with serious contagious diseases were quarantined, to protect the rest of the community.

A mother hurries a child past a quarantined house. The red cross indicates that the people inside may have the plague.

Thomas Moffet (1553–1604), an English scientist, drew pictures of fleas, lice, and mites. He even described the mite that causes scabies (a skin infection), and correctly identified sulfur as a way to combat the mite.

Athanasius Kircher (1601–1680), a German monk, looked through a crude microscope and saw "worms" in sour milk. He also noticed what he called "animalcula" in the blood of people who died from the bubonic plague.

Thomas Moffet, along with several other scientists, worked on this book. Although published after Moffet's death, it became the first natural history book printed in England.

Athanasius Kircher, a German monk, viewed microorganisms under an early microscope. He was among the first to believe that the plague was caused by these "animalcula."

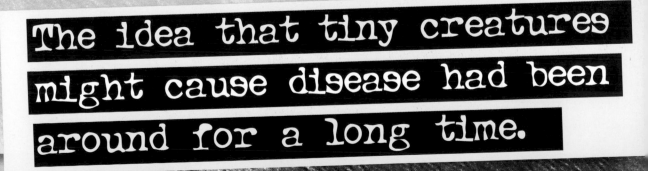

The idea that tiny creatures might cause disease had been around for a long time.

# THE FIRST MICROSCOPE: ANTONI VAN LEEUWENHOEK

Single-lens magnifying glasses had been around for thousands of years. Eventually, two lenses were used to make a crude microscope, but the poor quality of the lens created a blurry picture and magnified objects only 10 times their normal size.

Then came Antoni van Leeuwenhoek (1632–1723). He was a Dutch cloth merchant who hung drapes and sold buttons and sewing materials. But his hobby was grinding lenses. He became the best lens maker in Europe. He fashioned his masterful lenses into a microscope that could magnify objects nearly 300 times their normal size. He looked at many things under the microscope. His invention opened the door to a new world of knowledge. He observed bacteria and protozoa, which he called "very little animalcules." His careful observations showed bacteria in everything from ponds to human mouths.

Antoni van Leeuwenhoek's microscopes could magnify up to nearly 300 times, allowing him to see further into the microscopic world than anyone before him.

Italian biologist Marcello Malpighi used an early microscope to view human tissues. He published a book entitled *Anatome Plantarum*, which showed detailed drawings of human and plant anatomy.

Marcello Malpighi (1628–1694) was an Italian biologist who used the microscope to look specifically at human tissues. He saw the capillaries in lungs, nerve endings, brain tissue, and red blood cells. Malpighi made huge advances in the understanding of the human body, but jealous colleagues made his life miserable, even to the point of burning down his home. In 1691, the Pope asked him to be his personal physician, which was an extremely high honor.

# Early microscopes revealed bacteria and protozoa.

# CHILDBIRTH FEVER: IGNAZ SEMMELWEIS

**B**y the 1800s, only a few doctors believed that a healthy person could carry disease from one person to another. American writer and physician Oliver Wendell Holmes suggested that doctors who examined a sick person could carry a disease to a well person. However, his views were mostly dismissed as fantasy without proof.

Oliver
Wendell Holmes

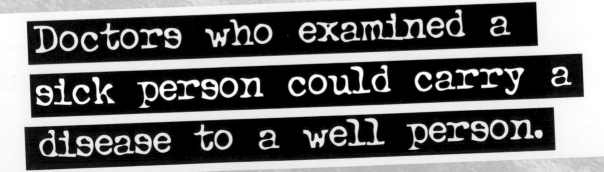

Doctors who examined a sick person could carry a disease to a well person.

Ignaz Semmelweis (1818–1865) was a German-Hungarian physician who worked in a hospital in Vienna, Austria. He was interested in a sickness called puerperal fever, or childbirth fever.

In those days, doctors didn't wash their hands before examining patients, and bed sheets were not washed regularly. Women giving birth were often particularly vulnerable to infection. This infection, called childbirth fever, was often fatal. Semmelweis saw that on the wards where doctors and apprentices worked, the childbirth fever death rate was as high as 20 percent. On the wards where midwives helped women give birth, the death rate from childbirth fever dropped to about 2 percent.

Semmelweis realized that the midwives did not examine many patients, and so didn't come into contact with sickness. The doctors, on the other hand, often arrived after treating sick patients, or even doing autopsies, and went right to examine women without washing their hands. While this practice seems horrifying to us today, people in those days did not understand germs or how diseases were transmitted.

Ignaz Semmelweis worked in a hospital where the childbirth fever death rate was as high as 20 percent. He noticed that it was common practice for doctors not to wash their hands after treating other sick patients. He believed that the doctors were transmitting diseases. Doctors, however, did not believe this was true.

Semmelweis insisted that doctors wash their hands in a solution of chlorinated lime water before examining other patients.

Semmelweis's suspicions were confirmed when a colleague accidentally cut his own finger during an autopsy. The colleague died a few days later of a sickness that seemed remarkably similar to childbirth fever.

In 1847, Semmelweis instituted a new hospital policy: doctors had to wash their hands before and after every examination. All the medical staff protested this policy, but Semmelweis held firm. As a result, the hospital's childbirth fever rate dropped to one percent. For the first time, science had proved a connection between infection and antiseptic (germ-killing) procedures.

The rest of Ignaz Semmelweis's story wasn't as happy. Semmelweis's boss, the director of the hospital, demoted him for his strange theories. Other doctors ridiculed his findings. They were upset at Semmelweis's idea that it was the doctors themselves who transmitted the infections. Despite clear evidence, the doctors refused to wash their hands.

The brilliant Semmelweis, who was an intense and sometimes unlikable man, was eventually imprisoned. He died in 1865, ironically, of an infection.

Despite the awful response to Semmelweis's ideas, he added one more piece of information to the germ puzzle. More and more doctors began to see that bloodletting was a waste of time, and that something besides "too much blood" might be the cause of sickness.

Semmelweis's theories offended doctors in the 1800s. They did not want to think that they could be the reason their patients got sick and even died. It would be many years before Semmelweis would be proved absolutely correct.

# ANTISEPTIC PROCEDURES: JOSEPH LISTER

English surgeon Joseph Lister noticed that an open wound often became infected. To stop these infections, he came up with a chemical spray made of carbolic acid that he called an "anti-septic."

In the 1860s, English surgeon Joseph Lister (1827–1912) worked in an important university hospital in Glasgow, Scotland. In general, the people in the university were open to new ideas, as opposed to the stubborn doctors that had worked with Ignaz Semmelweis.

Lister examined wounds, and the infections that emerged in some of them. He noticed that when a bone was broken but the skin wasn't cut, there was never an infection. But when the wound was exposed to the open air, such as in an amputation, infection (what they called "sepsis") very often occurred. He suspected something in the air caused the infection. He called it "disease dust."

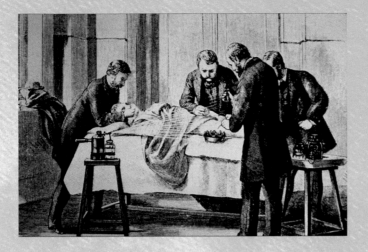

Lister had carbolic acid sprayed on the operating instruments, as well as all around the surgical area. It was a bad smell, but death rates from infections after surgery dropped from 45 percent to 15 percent.

Lister had read about the work of a French chemist named Louis Pasteur, who had suggested using heat or chemicals to kill microorganisms. Lister began spraying wounds and surgical instruments with a chemical called carbolic acid. The carbolic acid sterilized the wounds—it was an "anti-septic"—and death rates from infection after surgery plunged from 45 percent to 15 percent.

Most doctors in the world remained unconvinced. They were still suspicious of the idea that germs caused disease. But it was hard to argue with success. Slowly, over the next decades, doctors began to understand the importance of keeping wounds clean and sterile.

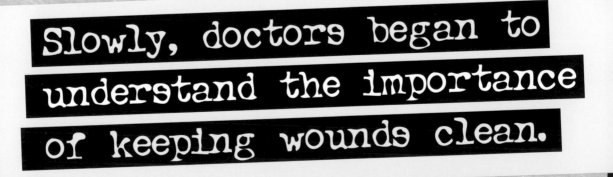

Slowly, doctors began to understand the importance of keeping wounds clean.

# THE BIG BREAKTHROUGHS: LOUIS PASTEUR

It's hard to exaggerate how much Louis Pasteur (1822–1895) did for medicine and biology in the mid- to late-1800s. Pasteur was a French chemist who accomplished many medical breakthroughs. He was not only a brilliant scientist himself, but he was able to build on the work of Lister, Semmelweis, Leeuwenhoek, Malpighi, and many others.

## The Function of Bacteria

Up until Pasteur's time, people were aware of protozoa and bacteria, but there was little understanding of what these tiny creatures did. Pasteur's early research dealt with the fermentation process of alcohol. He realized that it was these tiny microbes that caused fermentation. He also identified the reason that bread rises—tiny microbes called yeast.

# Pasteurization

In his early experiments with wine, Pasteur found that briefly heating the wine killed the microbes responsible for fermentation. This made the wine more resistant to spoiling. This process, called *pasteurization* in honor of Pasteur, is widely used today in many products.

# Vaccines for Rabies, Anthrax, and Other Diseases

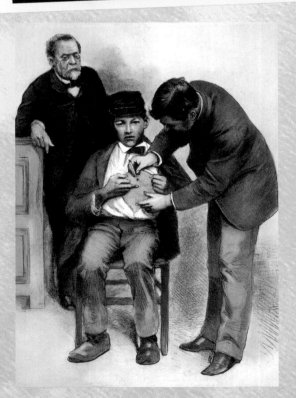

In 1885, Pasteur was working on a vaccine for rabies when authorities brought him a boy who had been bitten by a rabid dog. Without treatment, the boy would have surely died. Pasteur gave him the experimental vaccine, and the boy lived.

In 1885, Louis Pasteur gave Joseph Meister an experimental rabies vaccine. The 9-year-old, who had been bitten by a rabid dog, lived.

# The Death of Spontaneous Generation

People had always wondered why foods decay. If a piece of meat lies in the open air, flies and maggots will eventually start feeding on it. Some people in Pasteur's time believed that the maggots would just suddenly emerge on the meat. In other words, life arose out of nothing. This was called spontaneous generation. Pasteur was able to prove that the maggots got there when flies laid eggs in the meat. Through careful experimentation, he was able to prove that life comes from life—it does not emerge spontaneously. The theory of spontaneous generation had been falling out of favor, but Pasteur's experiments put the final nail in the coffin of that theory.

Fly larvae, or maggots, emerge after two or three days on a piece of ham. Pasteur proved that the maggots got there when flies laid eggs in the meat.

# The Germ Theory of Disease

Pasteur wasn't the first person to propose the theory that germs caused diseases, but it was his experiments that made others believe it. He was able to explain the results of Lister and Semmelweis. Sometimes, Pasteur is called the "Father of Germ Theory," since his work was so important in proving it.

One of Pasteur's famous experiments disproved the idea that bad air caused contaminations and infections. He constructed a glass flask with an S-shaped tube on top. Inside the flask was a nutrient solution that changed color if bacteria grew in it. The S-shaped tube was open to the air on one side, and connected to the flask on the other side. First, Pasteur boiled the solution inside the flask in order to kill any bacteria in the solution. Then, he waited.

Since the S-shaped tube was open on one side, air could get into the nutrient solution. If bad air caused infections, then the nutrient solution in the flask would become contaminated and change color. However, if bacteria were the cause of infection, as Pasteur suspected, then bacteria would not get to the solution. Since bacteria are heavier than air, they wouldn't be able to get through the curves in the tube.

As it turned out, the experiment showed that the solution remained free of bacteria, proving Pasteur's theory. Bacteria were the cause of infection, not bad air or spontaneous generation.

Pasteur always said, "Chance favors the prepared mind." His life was testament to that proverb. His mind was always prepared—ready to take his creativity and intellect and apply it to real-world problems.

# THE FATHER OF MICROBIOLOGY:
# ROBERT KOCH

Robert Koch is sometimes known as the "Father of Microbiology." He identified the bacteria that caused tuberculosis and cholera. His work helped thousands of people. Koch was awarded the Nobel Prize in 1905.

German physician Robert Koch (1843–1910) is sometimes called the "Father of Microbiology" because of his contributions to the field. Koch identified the bacteria that caused tuberculosis and cholera, both very dangerous diseases at the time. He experimented with different kinds of germs and how they caused different kinds of symptoms. He is also credited with making great strides in how to slice and stain bacteria cultures so they can be viewed under a microscope.

Koch is famous for his philosophy of how to determine which germs cause which diseases. These are called "Koch's Postulates," and they helped doctors understand germ theory.

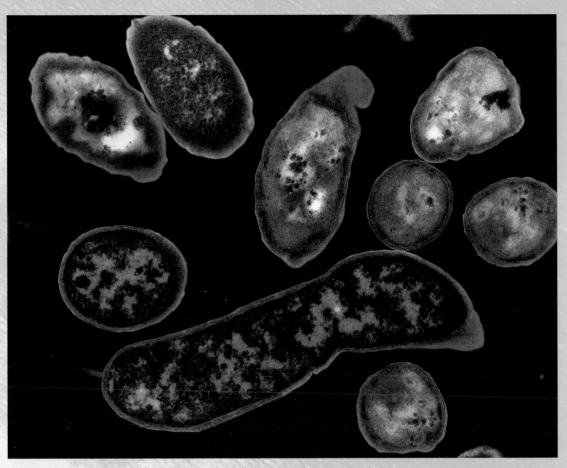

A *Vibrio cholerae* bacterium causes cholera in humans. People get cholera by drinking contaminated water. Cholera infects the intestine, causing vomiting and diarrhea. Patients may die from severe dehydration.

In 1883, Koch went to Egypt to help out with a cholera epidemic, where he learned about the bacteria. When the epidemic was over, he went to India, where cholera was a chronic problem. There, he learned which bacteria caused cholera and how it was transmitted through drinking water.

Later, Koch went on to discover the causes of many diseases, including bubonic plague, leprosy, and malaria. Koch won the Nobel Prize in 1905 for his discoveries about the disease tuberculosis.

# ANTIBIOTICS: ALEXANDER FLEMING

Alexander Fleming is best known for the 1928 discovery of penicillin. Penicillin worked to stop infections in deep wounds. Fleming's work helped save millions of people.

Scottish biologist Alexander Fleming (1881–1955) is best known for the 1928 discovery of penicillin, a drug that kills harmful bacteria.

Fleming went to medical school in London, England, graduating in 1906. He worked in battlefield hospitals in France during World War I (1914–1918). During the war, he learned that many soldiers survived their battlefield wounds, but died of septicemia, or infection, several days later. After the war, he searched for medicines that would cure infection. The antiseptics of World War I were not very effective, and only worked on a wound's surface. If a wound was deep, spraying an antiseptic into it could make things worse.

Colonies of bacteria susceptible to *Penicillium chrysogenum* radiate from the center of a petri dish. In 1928, Scottish bacteriologist Sir Alexander Fleming discovered that secretions from *Penicillium chrysogenum* destroyed colonies of the bacterium *Staphylococcus*.

In 1928, Fleming returned to his lab from a vacation. As an experiment, he had left several dishes sitting around the lab with various bacteria cultures growing in them. He realized that many of the dishes were contaminated with a fungus, which destroyed his experiment. He began to throw the dishes out, but then noticed in one dish an area around the fungus where bacteria did not grow. Fleming isolated the fungus and found it was from the *Penicillium* group, or genus.

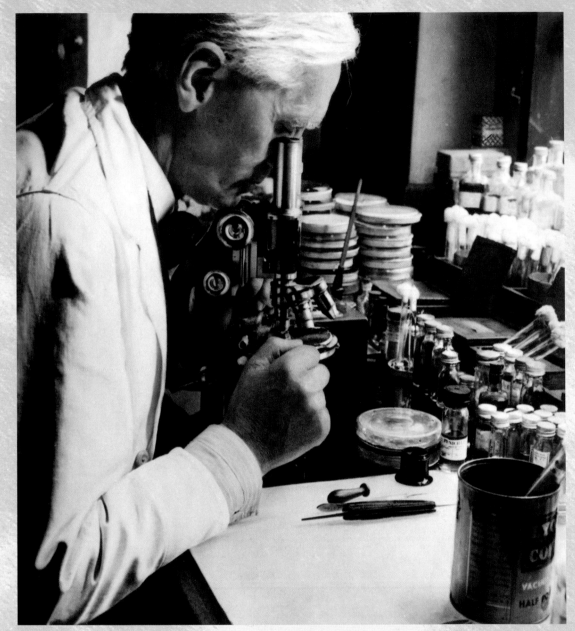

Fleming published his discovery in 1929, but most doctors ignored it. Some thought penicillin, the antibiotic made from the *Penicillium* fungus, might have some value as a topical antiseptic, but that's all. Fleming, however, believed that penicillin could also work inside the body. His experiments showed that the fungus had germ-killing power, even when it was diluted 800 times.

Fleming continued to try to cultivate penicillin, but it was difficult to grow, and difficult to isolate the germ-killing agent. Fleming began to wonder if it would ever work. He continued trying to cultivate it until 1940.

By then, two other men had begun working on penicillin. German Chemist Ernst Chain discovered how to isolate and concentrate the germ-killing agent in penicillin. Australian pharmacologist Howard Florey understood how to mass-produce it. The U.S. and British governments, in the midst of World War II (1939-1945), were concerned about the need for antibiotics. They funded Florey and Chain, and penicillin became a wonder drug that cured many diseases. Fleming, Florey, and Chain shared the Nobel Prize in 1945.

Sir Alexander Fleming    Sir Howard Florey    Dr. Ernst Boris Chain

The fungus used to create penicillin.

The discovery of penicillin is sometimes called an accident. That is only half true. While it was unexpected, Alexander Fleming noticed the "accident" and understood its significance. It is another example of Louis Pasteur's proverb, "Chance favors the prepared mind." Fleming's mind was keen and prepared, and his discovery has saved millions of lives.

# GLOSSARY

**ANTIBIOTICS**

A class of medicines that kill harmful bacteria in the body. Antibiotics only kill bacteria, not viruses.

**ANTISEPTIC**

Combining of the words "anti," which means "against," and "septic," which means "infection." Antiseptics stop or hinder infection.

**BACTERIA**

Plural form of bacterium.

**BACTERIUM**

A single-celled organism. Many types of bacterium cause disease.

**BLOODLETTING**

The process of taking blood from people. From ancient times, this was believed to be a cure-all for disease and sickness.

**EPIDEMIC**

When a disease spreads across a wide region. For example, the disease smallpox was very contagious and could easily be caught by those nearby, in time spreading over large areas.

**FUNGI**

The plural form of fungus, a class of plant-like microbes.

**HUMORS**

According to an ancient view of disease, the human body had four fluids, called humors: blood, phlegm, yellow bile, and black bile.

**MICROBE**

An abbreviation of the word microorganism.

**MICROBIOLOGY**

The study of microbes.

**MICROORGANISM**

A word that describe the variety of one-celled and microscopic life.

**PASTEURIZATION**

The process of heating liquids to kill bacteria.

**PROTOZOA**

A class of single-celled microbes.

**SEPTIC, SEPSIS, OR SEPTICEMIA**

Words doctors used in the 1800s to describe infection.

**VACCINE**

A dead or weakened form of a germ, given to patients so that the immune systems of their bodies will later recognize and fight the live germ.

"Chance favors the prepared mind." —L. Pasteur

# INDEX